John Ruskin

Three Letters and an Essay 1836-1841

Found in his tutor's desk

John Ruskin

Three Letters and an Essay 1836-1841
Found in his tutor's desk

ISBN/EAN: 9783744718400

Printed in Europe, USA, Canada, Australia, Japan

Cover: Foto ©Thomas Meinert / pixelio.de

More available books at **www.hansebooks.com**

THREE LETTERS AND AN ESSAY. BY JOHN RUSKIN. 1836–1841. FOUND IN HIS TUTOR'S DESK.

"And the thoughts of youth are long, long thoughts."

PUBLISHED BY GEORGE ALLEN, LONDON & ORPINGTON. MDCCCXCIII.

EDITOR'S PREFACE

In the days when the Rev. Thomas Dale had a school in Grove Lane, Camberwell, he was, as well as a schoolmaster, a poet, author, and preacher. In 1835 he was presented to the living of St. Bride's, Fleet Street; in 1843, to a Canonry of St. Paul's; and he died in 1870, shortly after accepting the Deanery of Rochester.

Amongst his papers were some writings of John Ruskin, his pupil in Grove Lane and, later, at King's College. The earliest of these is an essay written the year before Mr. Ruskin went to Oxford; the others are letters from Rome, Lausanne, and Leamington. The interest of these papers is great. They belong to that period when Mr. Ruskin was trying his powers, when " Modern Painters " was taking form, and when some of the most perfect pieces of prose ever written were given to English readers. The hand of the master is

b

very visible in all these papers, though the earliest
of them belongs to the days of boyhood.

Mr. Ruskin has given us in " Præterita " a
history of himself and of all the influences which
aided in the development of his powers. There
is about these recollections a calm clearness, an
acceptance of facts as they were, without either
railing against them or gilding them. The writer
is amused as he looks back down the vista of years
and recalls what the little boy in the blue shoes
thought ; what most appealed to the mind of the
schoolboy carrying his bag of books ; how the
devotion of his parents and the traditions of their
mode of life fenced him round ; how his mind kept
its own tendencies amongst all the training, and
went steadily forward, accumulating knowledge,
and growing towards the light. His was a
mind that never altered violently either its faith or
its opinions ; the matured fruit is not so dissimilar
to the bud and flower but that the process of
growth can be clearly traced without need of dis-
section or twisting of logic.

He writes of his schooldays in " Præterita " as
follows :—

" Meantime it having been perceived by my
father and mother that Dr. Andrews could neither

prepare me for the University nor for the duties of a bishopric, I was sent as a day-scholar to the private school kept by the Rev. Thomas Dale in Grove Lane, within a walking distance of Herne Hill. Walking down with my father after breakfast, carrying my blue bag of books, I came home to half-past one dinner, and prepared my lesson in the evening for the next day. Under these conditions I saw little of my fellow scholars, the two sons of Mr. Dale, Tom and James, and three boarders. . . . . I have already described in the first chapter of 'Fiction, Fair and Foul,' Mr. Dale's rejection of my clearly known grammar as a 'Scotch thing.' In that one action he rejected himself from being my master; and I thenceforward learnt all he taught me only because I had to do it."

The master, who, with the authority of his kind, thus wounded his pupil's feelings, was short, with thick hair, fair probably in those days, blue eyes, and firm square features. He was stern and impressive in manner. He was a man of power, an Evangelical leader, very much respected and admired by his following, but somewhat unbending in manner, austere to younger people, but withal generous and charitable beyond his means. He had also a keen sense of humour, though no one could have held "practical joking" in greater detestation.

This essay was either written for or submitted by the author to him in 1836, when Mr. Ruskin was sixteen or seventeen years old. To quote again from " Præterita " :—

" Some little effort was made to pull me together in 1836 by sending me to hear Mr. Dale's lectures at King's College, where I explained to Mr. Dale, on meeting him one day in the court of entrance, that porticoes should not be carried on the top of arches ; and considered myself exalted because I went in at the same door with boys who had square caps on. The lectures were on early English Literature, of which, though I had never read a word of any before Pope, I thought myself already a much better judge than Mr. Dale. His quotation of ' Knut the king went sailing by ' stayed with me, and I think that was all I learnt during the summer."

As the essay is not on early English Literature and has not been annotated or marked by the master, it was not apparently done as work for the course of lectures. It is, in fact, a glowing defence of the writer's favourite authors, Walter Scott,

Bulwer Lytton, and Byron. It begins logically and calmly, but as soon as the defence begins the champion draws his sword and falls fiercely on his opponents. He is a most gloriously enthusiastic partisan ; but the religious schools of that day dealt more hardly with the novelists, poets, and playwrights than they do now. In spite of his strong Evangelical bias, Mr. Dale was not among the decriers of fiction and poetry. Walter Scott was a favourite in his household ; there are no records of his feelings about Lytton's work, but Byron was an acknowledged great poet, sullied by the authorship of " Don Juan," a position the poet still holds in the majority of opinions. As soon as he could read, Mr. Ruskin tells us, Pope's Homer and the Waverley Novels became his regular week-day books, so his dictum on Sir Walter was the result of a considerable course of study taken by a small boy in his little chair in his own corner. Byron was also an old friend. The poems, including " Don Juan," were read by the elder Mr. Ruskin to his wife and son. He was a beautiful reader, and did justice to the music of the verse. There are not many who, writing at sixteen, can look back on so long and so cultivated an acquaintance with their favourite authors.

Mr. Ruskin matriculated at Christ Church, Oxford, in October 1836, and went into residence the following January. At the end of three years came a period of great disappointment and anxiety for himself and his friends. His health broke down and he was threatened with consumption. He went abroad for the winter of 1840–41, travelling with his parents and visiting Italy for the first time. His "severest and chiefly antagonist master" shared in the anxiety, and the two long letters from Rome and Lausanne were written to inform him of the state of his pupil's health. Perhaps the severity and antagonism revived in future discussions; certainly these letters are most friendly and confidential in tone; the regret for the exemplary goodness of his college days seems meant for sympathetic eyes. The writer's rapid, forcible description of the country he passes through, his impression of Chartres Cathedral, are all in the masterly style we connect with his name, wonderfully picturesque and vivid without ever being stiff or stilted. Not forgetful of the principal interest of his correspondent, he describes his impressions of the religious life of the country he travels through, writing from the Evangelical standpoint, from whence Mr. Ruskin has since moved, but which at that time was a subject of agreement between him and Mr. Dale. This is, therefore, a more correct description of his opinions at this time than any reminiscence can offer us, for the gradual alteration of opinions naturally softens the outline in retrospection, as the blue distance softens the mountains on the horizon.

His opinion of St. Peter's at Rome has not altered since this first impression more than fifty years ago, when the magnificence and barbarism of the great building is so forcibly expressed. Then comes a wonderfully vivid passage ; the description of that "strange horror" that to him overlay the whole city. One cannot but be thankful that it was not this paragraph that was mutilated in breaking the seal.

The cloud of ill-health and anxiety never left the travellers ; its shadow is in the next letter of six months after. During all this time that possible fatal development overhung the daily life of the parents and their only son. Still, in spite of the enforced care and seclusion, the time was by no means wasted. He saw and enjoyed Pompeii and went up Vesuvius, all his impressions and opinions being very similar to those he still expresses. The remarks on the Oxford Movement are particularly valuable, because one feels a natural curiosity as to how so powerful an influence affected the various thinkers then at the University. They are all the more interesting for the very reason that they do not contain a statement of opinion, but a simple account of the impression the men and their teaching made upon one who was at the same time tenacious of his views and unusually bold in facing difficulties. At this time, when a dreaded disease threatened him, his mind was evidently set on serious themes. The third letter, written from Leamington, discusses a question of conscience. The writer sets himself to argue out his difficulty with the evident intention of taking holy orders if he should be assured that such was the duty of a man in his position, bound by no necessity to work for his bread, and having the responsibility of preaching the gospel for the saving of souls. What the answer was we do not know, but we know the result. This is the last of the long letters. The others are short notes of no interest, though showing evidence that the discussions were not at an end.

Sydney Smith was a canon with Mr. Dale at St. Paul's, and, speaking of " Modern Painters," Mr.

Ruskin tells us :—"In the literary world, attention was first directed to the book by Sydney Smith, in the hearing of my severest and chiefly antagonist master, the Rev. Thomas Dale, who, with candid kindness, sent the following note of the matter to my father :—

"'You will not be uninterested to hear that Mr. Sydney Smith (no mean authority in such cases) spoke in the highest terms of your son's work, on a public occasion, and in presence of several distinguished literary characters. He said it was a work of transcendent talent, presented the most original views and the most elegant and powerful language, and would work a complete revolution in the world of taste. He did not know when he said this how much I was interested in the author!'"

HELEN PELHAM DALE.

June, 1893.

PUBLISHER'S NOTES

For the convenience of the reader—whether or not he be already in touch with Mr. Ruskin's matured writings, of which this little volume contains assuredly some of the earliest-recorded germs of thought emanating from the author's boyish mind—it has been deemed expedient to append a list of those works of Mr. Ruskin's which contain the expansion of the various axioms laid down and arguments brought forward in these Juvenilia, which, as the editor's preface tells us, were addressed to the man whose influence, especially in literary matters, had some considerable part in the formation of his pupil's mind.

In connection with the essay "Does the perusal of works of fiction act favourably, or unfavourably, on the moral character?" references should be made to Mr. Ruskin's amplifications of the subject, as well as his desultory allusions in such works as "Modern Painters," "Fors Clavigera," "On the Old Road" (more particularly the articles on "Fiction, Fair and Foul"), "Elements of Drawing" (in the appendix on "Things to be Studied"), "Munera Pulveris" (the chapter on "Government"), "Sesame and Lilies," "Arrows of the Chace," "Præterita," "Love's Meinie," and "The Queen of the Air."

With regard to the various subjects touched upon in the first of the letters, dated from Rome, Dec. 31 (written in 1840), the reader will find it useful to refer to the following works :—

"The Two Paths," "Lectures on Art, 1870," "The Bible of Amiens," "Fors Clavigera," "Modern Painters," and works dealing more particularly with Italian art, such as "Val d'Arno," "Ariadne Florentina," and "Mornings in Florence." To pick out special portions of the letter for remark would be making invidious distinctions; but there are noteworthy points in the writer's description of the Mediterranean coast—his impressions of Rome, and the Italian peasantry ("neither fish nor flesh, neither noble nor fisherman," as he described the population of Venice later on in "Fors Clavigera," vol. v.

letter 49)—and the expression of his strong sense of the evils of "cramming" for University honours, afterwards endorsed more emphatically in the appeal to parents, in the closing sentences of the Lecture on Serpents ("Deucalion," pt. 7).

The second letter (dated six months later) contains, *inter alia*, what—to readers of Mr. Ruskin's later eulogiums of Italy—will come as an astounding piece of news—his assertion that "the climate of Italy never did agree with me ; " also a remark, by the way, on the submission of Newman (the late Cardinal Newman) " to his Bishop in the affair of the Tracts," which leads to a dissertation on the then burning question of the day and the various classes of disputants—interesting for its evidence of the young writer's growing doubts of the infallibility of that Evangelical school in whose dogmas he had been brought up. His remarks on his parents' experiences, as well as his own, of the Protestant churches in Italy, remind one of the crisis in his life—upon which he has dwelt so strongly and repeatedly in " Præterita," " Fors Clavigera," and elsewhere—on that Sunday in 1858 when he turned from the little Waldensian chapel in Turin, for an hour's meditation in the gallery " where Paul Veronese's 'Solomon¨and the Queen

of Sheba' glowed in full afternoon light," and felt
that "that day my Evangelical beliefs were put
away, to be debated of no more" (" Præterita,"
vol. iii. chap. i.).

In the third letter, written from Leamington in
Sept. 1841, we have the embryo of ideas which
expanded later on into the "Notes on the Con-
struction of Sheepfolds"; the "Letters on the
Lord's Prayer"; the politico-economical question
raised in "Fors Clavigera," with its passionate
appeal (vol. v. letter 58)—"What am I myself,
then, infirm and old, who take, or claim, leadership
even of these lords? God forbid that I should
claim it ; it is thrust and compelled on me—utterly
against my will, utterly to my distress, utterly—in
many things—to my shame. But I have found no
other man in England, none in Europe, ready to
receive it, or even desiring to make himself capable
of receiving it. Such as I am, to my own amaze-
ment I stand—so far as I can discern—alone in
conviction, in hope, and in resolution, in the
wilderness of this modern school. Bred in luxury,
which I perceive to have been unjust to others,
and destructive to myself; vacillating, foolish, and
miserably failing in all my own conduct in life,
and blown about hopelessly by storms of passion

I, a man clothed in soft raiment, I, a reed
shaken with the wind, have yet this message to all
men again entrusted to me: 'Behold, the axe
is laid to the root of the tree. Whatsoever tree
therefore bringeth not forth good fruit, shall be
hewn down and cast into the fire.'" And the
later protest for leisure to pursue the line of work
which is peculiarly his own—" Here is a little grey
cockle-shell lying beside me, which I gathered, the
other evening, out of the dust of the island of St.
Helena, and a brightly spotted snail-shell, from
the thirsty sands of Lido; and I want to set myself
to draw these, and describe them, in peace.   Yes!
all my friends say, 'that is my business; why can't
I mind it, and be happy?'   Well, good friends,
I would fain please you, and myself with you; and
live here in my Venetian palace, luxurious;
scrutinant of dome, cloud, and cockle-shell. . . . .
But, alas! my prudent friends, little enough of all
that I have a mind to may be permitted me.   For
this green tide that eddies by my threshold is full
of floating corpses, and I must leave my dinner to
bury them, since I cannot save; and put my
cockle-shell in cap, and take my staff in hand, to
seek an unencumbered shore" (" Fors Clavigera,"
vol. vi. letter 72).   Also the sense of greater

responsibility that there should be in the "highly bred and trained English, French, Austrian, or Italian gentleman (much more a lady)," who "will have some duties to do in return—duties of living belfry and rampart" ("Sesame and Lilies," Lecture I.), and, lastly, the foundation of the ethical part of his art teaching upon the formulæ, " Man's use and function are, to be the witness of the glory of God and to advance that glory by his reasonable obedience and resultant happiness," and " All great art is praise," constantly dwelt upon throughout such works as " Modern Painters," "The Laws of Fésole," " Aratra Pentilici," " The Eagle's Nest," "Lectures on Art, 1870," and " The Art of England."

ESSAY ON LITERATURE

A

ESSAY ON LITERATURE—1836

Does the perusal of works of fiction act favourably or unfavourably on the moral character?

IT is necessary, in the consideration of such a question as this, to be particularly careful to permit our judgment to be altogether unbiassed by our feelings, and to divest ourselves entirely of that weakness of mind which disposes us to yield to our wishes rather than our reason, to believe in the existence of that which we desire to exist, in the validity of the arguments which we desire to be valid, and in the fallacy of the statements which we hope may be false. For our

feelings naturally incline us to hope that
we may not be able to prove that writings from which we have derived incal-
culable enjoyment are injurious and immoral, and our wishes rise up in opposition to our judgment; they remonstrate
against the investigation, they deprecate
the decision, they beseech, they implore,
that employments so delightful may not
be condemned for the past nor forbidden
for the future; and that hours whose
wings were loaded with odours so soft,
and tinted with colours so gay, may not
be pronounced to have left darkness in
the eyes they have dazzled, or pestilence
in the air they have enchanted.

But it is necessary that such feelings
should have no voice in our inquiry after
truth, and that our wishes, as they have
no inflence over facts, should have none
over our opinions. Our judgment must

be armed with despotic power, and not
a syllable of remonstrance be permitted,
even if we think that power tyrannically
or unjustly directed.

Yet, on the other hand, we hope,
gentle reader, that you are gentle—that
you are not one of those philosophers,
falsely so named, who assert, in the teeth
of reason, and to the injury of the cause
of religion, that whatever is amusing
must be criminal ; that a grave countenance and severe demeanour are the true
signs of sanctity of mind and consequent
morality of conduct ; that austerity is the
companion of innocence, and gloom of
religion. We have been taught a different lesson by a higher authority : we
know that morality may be radiant with
smiles and robed in rejoicing ; and we
do not deprecate, because we despise,
the objections of those who affirm that

all pleasure is necessarily evil, and all enjoyment inevitably crime.

Mental recreation is felt to be sometimes necessary by the best and the wisest. Whatever be the rapidity of the race in the path of right, breath must be sometimes taken ; whatever be the ardour of the search after knowledge, repose must be sometimes courted. When the brain is confused with the intricacy of investigation, and the reason fatigued with the labour of argument ; when the brilliancy of thought is darkened, and the energies of the mind failing, and the strength of the judgment impaired, what recreation can be more exhilarating or delightful than to enwreathe ourselves with the imagination of the poet, or mingle amongst the creations of the romancer ? The mind is released from the severity of confinement without being lost in the infinity of useless reverie, and invigorated by a moving repose, not weakened by a drowsy and unthinking inanity.

We may therefore pronounce such productions to be useful if we can prove them not to be injurious, and we have some slight hope of being able to claim for them at least this small advantage.

But we do begin to feel nervous in our optics, for lo, fearful visions arise upon our sight, and terrified in our tympanum, for awful sounds are bursting upon our ears. We behold through a mist of awe, through an atmosphere of consternation, Quaker ladies shaking their heads at us, old maids their sticks at us, crabbed old gentlemen their fists at us, and ugly (by courtesy plain) young ladies their tongues at us. Here's a pretty mess we have got into! Gruff,

shrill, squeaking, whistling—the voices
of multitudinous discord astonish our
nerves : " How false! how untenable!
how shocking! how immoral! how
impious!" Here's a climax! We have
raised the wind, we think we have
untied the bags of Ulysses ; we have
called spirits from the vasty deep. Oh,
ye poor works of fiction, verily ye are
in a woeful plight, for overwhelming is
the number and inveterate the hostility
of your enemies. There is the old maid
of jaundiced eye and acidulated lip,
whose malice-inwoven mind looks on all
feelings of affection and joy as the
blight looks on the blossom ; whose
sweetest food is the disappointment,
whose greatest delight is in the grief,
whose highest exultation is in the crime
of the younger and happier ; who masks
malice of heart under sanctification of

countenance, and makes amends for the
follies of her youth by making her
parrot say "Amen" to her prayers.
There is the haughty and uncharitable
sectarian who stalks through the world
with scorn in his eye and damnation on
his tongue. There are home-bred
misses who have set up for being
pious because they have been set down
as being ugly (on the principle which
makes nunneries the scarecrow deposi-
tories of Catholic countries), and en-
rapture their pa's and ma's by becoming
"occasional contributors" to some very
moral and excellent juvenile miscellany,
of which they regularly favour the January number with some very sagacious remarks on "The Rapid Flight of Time,"
in which they give their readers the very
valuable, interesting, and novel information that 1835 came before 1836, and

that the next year to 1836 will be 1837, concluding, by way of pathos, with the very original idea that all mortals are mortal, and that as soon as people are born it becomes likely that, some time or other, they will die. Or else, by way of being philosophical, they indulge us with essays on "Novel Reading"— precious pieces of business, quite gems in their way—consisting of amiable dia- logues between good boys and girls— Fanny and Emmy, William and George —in which every sentence is composed of very fine, wise-looking words, sought for with much care through the pages of the well-thumbed dictionary. We do remember us of some of these most exquisite compositions, and we own that a tremor ran through us as we did peruse, that our spectacles shook upon our nose, and our hairs, quitting the recumbent position upon our forehead to which age and wisdom had long inclined them, began to assume, through fear for the reputations of Scott and Bulwer, the semblance of that spruce, upward inclination which rendered us in our youth so irresistible. For great, indeed, was our terror lest the names of these unfortunate authors should be over-whelmed by the weight of such authority, and their fame withered for ever by the force of such rhetoric and the severity of such criticism.

We were much too humble, in the first stun of our astonishment, to venture into combat with champions of such prowess, but on time being given us to breathe, we began to opine that there might be some points of weakness open to our attack—some feeble syllogisms which might be invalidated. We therefore beg thee, gentle reader, to submit to a recapitulation of some of these most exquisite arguments.

One of the first which we remember was a remark that, as all such works were confessedly fictitious, it was quite shocking to sit down deliberately to the perusal of a continued tissue of false-hoods.   We should like to know from what flinty numskull this most brilliant spark of witticism has been elicited.   We hope that this most puissant upholder of truth is convinced that the existence of his own veritable codshead is no "tissue of falsehood."   We might take the trouble (and with a person of so bright an intellect it might not be inconsider-able) to teach him the difference between falsehood and imagination.   (Indeed, as it is certain that no one can form an idea of sights he has not seen, or feelings he has not felt, and as, in all probability, this specimen of human sagacity might have his total allowance of brains chopped up, washed, pickled, and evaporated, without one drop of imagination being distilled from the *caput mortuum*, it might be almost impossible to hammer into him the slightest idea of what this impalpable property might be.) We might inform his simplicity that the characters in works of fiction are representatives of men in general, are persons who have existed and will exist again, modified only by the manners prevailing at certain periods, doing what has been done, feeling what has been felt, thinking what has been thought, and will be done, felt, and thought again. We might, by way of example, hold up before his nose the decidedly and professedly moral fictions of the Edgeworth and Sherwood school, and we could bring up the overwhelming examples of fictions and fables being used in pages of a very different character. But we will not insult our readers by appearing to think it necessary to prove to them the absurdity of such an objection. We shall proceed to his next argument, in which Master Slender ventures to particularise upon us, to enunciate by name the "bears i' the town," which the dogs, he himself included, make such a howling about. As Scott, then, has been named by our antagonists, we will take him and Bulwer as the heads of two different lines of fiction, and to them will we apply in succession, and by their works will we try the arguments of our opponents.

We have heard it said that Scott's historical romances gave false ideas of history.

Now we maintain, on the contrary, that
a more better and distinct idea, not only
of historical events, but of national feeling
at the time, will be gained, and has been
gained, by most persons, from Scott's
novels than from any dry and circum-
stantial history. For history can only
'detail the principal events of the time
(accompanied, perhaps, with imperfect,
though masterly, sketches of character) ;
it gives us only the skeleton of past times,
which the works of the great novelist
clothe for us with flesh and blood, and
endow with life and motion ; he gives us
the various minute traits by which party
feeling was exhibited, and the delicate
distinctions of character which were
observable in the men of the day, and
he does so in the only manner in which,
effectually, it can be done, by exhibit-
ing them under everyday circumstances,

and he does this invariably with truth—truth ascertained by his laborious research and almost illimitable historical knowledge. Take "Woodstock" for an example—we are certain that a person who had once read it with care would have clearer ideas of the characters of Charles and Cromwell, of the degrees of party feeling prevalent at the time, of the manner in which they were exhibited by the members of the opposing factions, and of the general state of the country and the people, than could be obtained by the most laborious research into all the volumes of history that ever were or will be written, and what is more, he might depend upon his ideas being true, for Scott never suffers his party feeling to have much to do with the representation of his historical characters. We would likewise ask the readers of the

"Last Days of Pompeii" if they have not a clearer idea of the manners prevailing at the period than they ever obtained from their classical studies. We wish we had space and time to detail and illustrate this advantage of historical novels more fully, and urge it more weightily; but as it refers only to their utility, and has nothing to do with the question in discussion, namely, their morality, we are compelled to pass on to another objection of our opponents, which at the first glance appears a little more weighty than any they have hitherto advanced. We have frequently heard it said that Scott held up to ridicule the religious principles of the Puritans and Covenanters of old times, and exhibited them as absurd, ridiculous, and despicable in their fanaticism. Now we assert, that nothing could

B

prove more certainly than such an objection the bad hearts and weak judgments of those by whom it is advanced. In the very first pages of "Old Mortality" we are prejudiced in favour of the Covenanters by the beautiful description of the character and occupation of the good old man from whom the work is named, and through the whole of the novel we are certain that, although the expressions and habits of the Covenanters may occasionally excite a smile, their characters and feelings will always induce respect in the mind of a man of either judgment or feeling. It has been said that Scott misrepresented them, but there is no misrepresentation in the case ; they were in reality such as they are exhibited in the romance ; and those persons who consider them ridiculous there, would have considered them

equally so had they held actual intercourse with them. For the man who
could treat with contempt or mockery
the character of Mause Hedrigg is one
whose limited faculties and despicable judgment enable him only to perceive the laughable misapplication of her
religious language and the dangerous
folly of her mistaken zeal, and who is
not capable of either perceiving, or
appreciating if he did perceive, the
inward beauty of character, the holiness
of mind, the fervour of devotion, which
separate her heart so entirely from the
earth, and enable her, with a high and
enduring heroism, to despise its good
and welcome its evil. The worldly man
and the weak man may cry out against
Scott for representing the Covenanters
as characters which appear fools—to the
one because he cannot appreciate, to the

other because he cannot fathom, the motives by which they are actuated. Let them know that Scott has represented the Covenanters as they were, and that what appears folly to the worldly wisdom of the one and the short-sighted intellect of the other, was felt by the author, and is felt by the readers who can understand him, to be fervid heroism and venerable piety.

The last argument against works of fiction which we remember is the weightiest, and because it is so, we put it in the forefront of the battle, for we wish to employ no artful concealments, no tricks of logic, no dexterities of disputation in our search after truth. It is said that the perusal of works of fiction induces a morbid state of mind, a desire for excitement, and a languor if it be withheld, which is highly detrimental both to its intellectual powers and its morality. Now intoxication is detrimental to the health, but a moderate use of wine is beneficial to it ; and voracity in works of fiction is detrimental to the mind, but moderation, we hope to prove, is beneficial to it, and much better than total confinement to the thick water-gruel of sapient, logical and interminable folios.

We will endeavour, therefore, to trace the effect of the works of Scott upon the mind, and we affirm, first, that they humanize it ; secondly, that they cultivate and polish it ; and thirdly, and consequently, improve its moral feelings.

First, they humanize it. The descriptions of scene and character in Scott are so vivid that they have the same effect upon us as if we actually passed through them. We hold intercourse with an infinite variety of characters, and that under peculiarly favourable circumstances, for their thoughts and the motives of their actions are laid open to us by the author ; we perceive where they mistake and where they do wrong, we behold the workings of their feelings and the operation of their reason, and we see that according to the justice and wisdom of the means pursued is the success obtained.   For Scott is beautifully just in his awards of misfortune and success, and throughout all his works there is no instance of any evil happening to any character which has not been incurred by his own fault or folly. Again, all our good feelings are brought into play ; no one ever envies the hero of a romance ; selfishness is put entirely out of the question ; we feel as if we were the air, or the wind, or the light, or the heaven, or some omnipresent, invisible thing that had no interests of its own. We become, for the time, spirits altogether benevolent, altogether just, hating vice, loving virtue, weeping over the crime, exulting in the just conduct, lamenting the misfortune, rejoicing in the welfare of others. Is this no advance in morality? Have we not for the time overcome, or, rather, driven away our great enemy, Self? Have we not become more like the angels? Are not our emotions sweeter, our hopes purer, our tears holier, when they are felt for others, nourished for others, wept for others? Every one must acknowledge that a continuance of such utterly unselfish feelings of love and universal benevolence must be beneficial, must be humanizing, to the mind by which they are experienced.

Secondly, they cultivate and polish

the mind.   Not only are we made to know the world, as it is called, by passing through an infinite variety of scenes and circumstances, but we are endowed, in acquiring this knowledge, with a transcendent and infinitely superior intellect—that of the author. For he who carries us through the scenes, gives us his remarks upon them as he goes on, yet in such a way that we fancy they are originally, what they eventually become, our own thoughts upon the subject.   We thus look at things with an eye whose glance is far more lynx-like, whose specu-lation far more fierily brilliant than our own ; our opinions are sculptured into more accurate forms, our judgment is guided, our reason directed, our in-tellect made more keen.   We are thus rendered fit to hold intercourse with the

characters of the tale, and this, we should
remember, is both an honour and an advantage, for those persons, when represented in a favourable light, are endowed with all the superior mind of him
whose imaginings they are. Luminous in
their thoughts, quick in their wits, delightful in their conversation, brave in
their hearts, moral in their feelings,
their society is an advantage which
would be sought with the utmost avidity
in the world of reality, and must be pro-
ductive of the greatest benefit in that of
fiction. We do not insist upon the
benefit to be derived, in the shape of
knowledge of the world, from our intercourse in such works with all sorts of
men, for we are not speaking of the ac-
quisition of worldly wisdom, but of the
improvement of the mind, which,
thirdly, we affirmed to be the result of

the perusal of Scott's works. We have proved it to be humanized, we have proved it to be cultivated, polished, and refined ; it is therefore improved. Its moral principles and benevolent feelings have been as much encouraged as its selfishness has been neutralized. This effect has been accompanied with a sharpening of intellect and an accession of ideas, and this has been accomplished, not by severe study, or intense thought, but by the repose of a wearied brain and the relaxation of a leisure hour.

We have not spoken of Scott's poetical fiction, because we are about to review the dangers and the benefits of this species of composition as united in the works of a poet of more meteorical talent and more evil fame. Let us, however, before leaving the works of Scott, remark that their tendency

is always moral : guilt is always
punished and virtue always rewarded,
and, *vice versâ*, virtue never suffers and
guilt never prospers. His characters
are perfect examples. Those of women
are, in particular, beautifully drawn ; indeed, they are, with few exceptions, so
prudent and exemplary as to be detrimental to his novels in two ways : they
render them, first, less interesting and,
secondly, less natural. They render
them less interesting, because we have
not the slightest fear for such sage,
amiable creatures—such faultless para-
gons ; we see they never have got into
a scrape, and we are sure they never
will. Whether, by making his heroines
so prudent, he has rendered his tales less
natural, we leave to the judgment of
those who have more knowledge of the
sex than our bachelor experience can

boast of, but we are certain that the influence of such beautiful examples must be highly beneficial to those who attempt to imitate them.

We will next endeavour to trace the effect upon the mind of the works of another author who is at the head of the modern metaphysical and sentimental school of fiction. But we shudder at our own temerity, for we feel that by the enunciation of the last adjective we have raised up in opposition to us another and a more awful regiment of enemies —the anti-sentimentalists. We shall have fashionable tailors, *à la mode* snips, snapping their shears and kicking their cross legs in our faces; we shall have 'prentice barbers stropping their saponaceous intellects to come to the brush with us. Every small wit that ever fancied himself sage, every goose that ever cackled with an air, every blind owl that has ever attempted to look wise, has thought fit to signalise his sagacity by turning up his snub nose at sentiment. A kind of running giggle echoes in our ears whenever we pronounce the word—goosified and idiotical enough, but yet meant to testify the wisdom of the gigglers. We have seen grave sneers, too, always of course from persons who had not soul enough in their mutton and beef bodies to make a pennyweight of sentiment. We remember a moral essayist, who, after a few very interesting truisms, began the subject-matter of his discourse with, "I am no sentimentalist." We could have told him so from the first stupidities of his pen. We knew he had not one gleam of idea bright enough to enable him even to understand—much less to be—a sentimentalist. He and his brother abusers of sentiment put us in mind of the toad who, having been immured in a block of sandstone for 3000 years, was found on its liberation engaged in writing its autobiography, in which it had very satisfactorily proved the absurdity of supposing that light and colour were either useful or beautiful.

Yet we are not speaking in defence of the boarding-school misses' rural, romantic, " La Ma !" and " Gracious Pa ! " sort of sentiment, nor of that of the poetical haberdashers, who having been captivated by the slender fingers and radiant smile of some nymph of the counter engaged in measuring out a yard of tape, go down to Margate or Ramsgate to eat shrimps, read " Romeo and Juliet," do the despairing lover, and get the colic ; nor of that of elegant lawyers' clerks, who, having obtained a fortnight's leave of absence, are brought down (nearly bringing themselves up on the way) per steamer to Edinburgh, and then, the " Lady of the Lake " in their pocket and a brand new silk umbrella in their hand, perambulate, with open mouth and upturned eyes, the "hawful shoeblimities" of the Scotch Highlands.

Nor are we defending the sentiment of poetasters who bore Spring, Summer, Autumn, and Winter with interminable sonneteering, and never see the moon without putting "thou" before it, thus compounding the pretty piece of sentiment " Thou Moon."

Nor, finally, are we defending the Charlotte and Werther, bread-and-butter sort of sentiment. But we are speaking of what we may call, translating the Latin derivative into English, real, refined feeling, such as that which is so conspicuous in the works of the author we are about to bring forward—Mr. Bulwer.

The sentiment of this author is as philosophical as that of Adam Smith, but the latter writer gives us only the mechanics of feeling. In the works of Bulwer we have their life and poetry ; the one gives us the automaton of feeling, the other its soul. His writings are full of an entangled richness of moving mind, glittering with innumerable drops of rosy and balmy and quivering dew, instinct with a soft, low, thrilling whisper of thought, like that which the young fairies hear from the green grass and kind flowers as they grow, and change, and sigh, beneath the hushed light of the star-inwoven noon of night, and we listen to the low voice of his musing until it melts away into our spirit, as if its sweet harp-like music rose up out of our own mind, as if its mysterious flowing were from the deep fountains of our own heart. Bulwer's descriptions are always beautiful ; he not only sees, himself, but he teaches us to see like him. The language in which he describes is burning, because every word has its own half hinted, deep laid, beautiful thought, which he leaves us, as he floats on amidst the calm but beaming æther of his own imagination, to follow, and follow afar, until we are lost in a wilderness of sweet dreaming. He gives Nature a spirit that she had not before. The earth, and the air, and the leaves, and the waves, and the clouds, are all endowed by him with voices ; he makes us feel them with our eyes like visible emotions ; he makes them each touch a

c

chord in our heart with their gentle
fingers, and then lifts up the weak
melody, and follows its tremulous vibra-
tion till he arouses deeper tones and
melancholy memories, and visions half
sad but most beautiful.   He has not one-
fifth of the invention of Scott, but he
has, in one respect, more imagination,
yet a kind of imagination which it is
difficult to explain.   He endows inani-
mate things with more life, more spirit,
and he revels in the deep waters of the
human heart, where all is seen misty
and dim, but most beautiful, by the pale
motion of the half lost light of the out-
ward sun through the softly sobbing
waves of our thoughts.   The perusal
of his works, or of works like them,
must always refine the mind to a great
degree, and improve us in the science
of metaphysics.   The general movements

of the mind may be explained in theories
and investigated by philosophers, but
there are deep-rooted, closely entangled
fibres which no eye can trace, no thought
can find, yet they may be felt if touched
by a skilful hand.

Whether the increase of our delicacy
of feeling improves the mind in a moral
point of view, is a difficult question, but
we are inclined to think that it does.
The more we can feel, the more beauty
we shall perceive in this universal frame.
No man knows how lovely Nature
is who has not entwined her with his
heart, and caused parts of her glory to
be capable of awakening peculiar, asso-
ciated lines of thought in his own mind,
and the feeling of her beauty is a
decidedly moral feeling, and very beneficial to the mind. It might be thought
that what we have been saying of

Bulwer's works might have been said of all poetry, but this is not the case; it could only have been said of poetical prose, and we will let him tell the reason in his own words. " Verse cannot contain the refining and subtle thoughts which a great prose writer embodies : the rhyme eternally cripples it ; it properly deals with the common problems of human nature which are now hackneyed, and not with the nice and philosophising corollaries which may be drawn from them : thus, though it would seem at first a paradox, commonplace is more the element of poetry than of prose " (" Pilgrims of the Rhine ").

Yet although prose is thus more refined, poetry is the most inspiring, and our task would not be completed unless we endeavoured also to trace the effect of poetical fiction on the mind.   But our

time is nearly exhausted, we are fatigued
of the subject ; we feel as if we had been
uttering nothing but truisms, convicting
of absurdity objections which no one
ever supposed to be reasonable, proving
the truth of reasons whose truth was
never doubted, and the beneficial influence of that whose beneficial influence
was never disputed. We feel as if we
had been beating the air—contending,
but with no opponent—struggling, but
with no impediment. But when we pronounce the name of " The Bride of
Abydos," we feel that the case is altered.
The dust and ashes of criticism become
living before our eyes, and a murmur of
indignation arises from the multitudes of
crawling things. But the name hath
touched us with its finger, and our brain
is burning, our heart is quivering, our
soul is full of light. Oh, the voice, the

glory, the life, that breathes through the bursts of melody which fall upon our ear! Oh, what a heaven of agonised spirit was that, whose night was so meteored with the rush of its inspiration, glorious with the melancholy light of its cold stars and its pale planets, soft with the gentleness of its dew, terrible in the boundless eternity of its darkness! We have known minds, and great ones too, which were filled with such a horror of Byron's occasional immorality, as to be unable to separate his wheat from his chaff —unable to bask themselves in the light of his glory, without fearing to be scorched by his sin. These we have pitied, and they deserve pity, for they are debarred from one of the noblest feasts that ever fed the human intellect. We do not hesitate to affirm that, with the sole exception of Shakespere, Byron was the greatest poet

BYRON 39

that ever lived, because he was perhaps
the most miserable man. His mind was
from its very mightiness capable of ex-
periencing greater agony than lower intellects, and his poetry was wrung out
of his spirit by that agony. We have
said that he was the greatest poet that
ever lived, because his talent was the
most universal. Excelled by Milton
and Homer only in the vastness of
their epic imaginations, he was excelled
in nothing else by any man. He was
overwhelming in his satire, irresistible
in the brilliancy of the coruscations of his
wit, unequalled in depth of pathos, or in
the melancholy of moralising contempla-
tion. We may challenge every satirist
and every comic poet that ever lived to
produce specimens of wit or of comic
power at all equal to some that might be
selected from " Don Juan." We might

challenge every lyric poet that ever
existed to produce such a piece of lyric
poetry as the

> " long, low island song
> Of ancient days, ere tyranny grew strong,"

which soothes the dying hour of Haidée.
Take (and we name them at random) the
death of Haidée, the dirge at the end
of " The Bride of Abydos," and " The
Dream," and match their deep, their
agonising pathos, if it be possible, from
the works of any other poet.   Take his
female characters from his tragedies—
and Shakespere will not more than
match   them — take   his   moralising
stanzas from " Childe Harold."   What
other   moralist   ever   felt   so   deeply ?
In every branch of poetry he is super-
eminent ; there is no heart whose peculiar tone of feeling he does not touch.

We have not words mighty enough to
express our astonishment—our admiration. Tell us not that such writing is
immoral; we know, for we have felt,
what a light of illimitable loveliness,
what a sickness of hushed awe, what a
fire of resistless inspiration, what a glory
of expansive mind fills the heart and
soul, as we listen to the swell of such
numbers ; there is a river of rushing
music that sweeps through our thoughts,
resistless as a whirlwind, yet whose
waves sing, as they pass onward, so
softly, so lowly, so holily, half-madden-
ing with their beauty of sweet sound,
until we are clasped in the arms of the
poetry as if borne away on the wings of
an archangel, and our rapture is illimitable, and we are elevated and purified
and ennobled by the mightiness of the
influence that overshadows us. There

is not, there cannot be, a human being "of soul so dead" as not to feel that he is a better man, that his ideas are higher, his heart purer, his feelings nobler, his spirit less bound by his body, after feeding on such poetry. But our enthusiasm has drawn us into a false inference. There *are* animals who neither have felt this inspiration themselves nor believe that others can feel it. They talk about Byron's immorality as if he were altogether immoral, and they actually appear to imagine that *they! they!!* yes, *they!!!* will be able to wipe away his memory from the earth. Our risibility has been excited by the Laird of Balmawhapple's humorous assertion of his dignity by discharging his horse-pistol against the crags of Stirling Castle; but this is but typical of the audacity of these pismires, these dogs that bay the moon, these foul snails that crawl on in their despicable malice, leaving their spume and filth on the fairest flowers of literature, but are inferior to the slug in this respect, that their slime can neither shine nor injure. It has been said that there is never anger where there is no fear ; but who does not feel indignation mingled with his scorn of these Grub Street reptiles, even although the dust of a single year will overwhelm them for ever, and the impotence of their life be equalled by the oblivion of their death !

EARLY LETTERS

ROME, *December* 31 (1840).

MY DEAR SIR,

I have delayed writing from day to day, first that I might have something to tell you of my health and, secondly, that I might not speak of this place under early and false impressions. For myself, I am certainly better, though much checked in all my pursuits from a little inconvenient roughness about the chest, which renders it improper for me to read or draw to any extent, or to do anything that requires stooping, and equally so to take violent or prolonged exercise, or to go out at night, or to

saunter in cold galleries, or to talk
much, or walk much, or do anything
"much," so that I am subject to perpetual mortification in taking care of an
absolute nothing, as far as it goes at
present. Still I am better here than I
should be at home, and there is a great
deal of information and pleasure to be
picked up bit by bit, if one is on the
watch for it. We sauntered leisurely
enough through France, taking some
six weeks from Calais to Nice, and
passing over most of the characteristic
portions of French landscape, the chalk
downs and fertile pasture valleys of
Normandy, the poplar plains and turreted
banks of the Loire, as far as Tours, then
the volcanic cliffs and black lavas of
Auvergne, the vineyards and fortresses
of the Rhone, the limestone peaks of
Vaucluse, and finally the loveliest

fragment of all France, where the Basses
Alpes throw out their promontories,
clothed from base to summit with an
unbroken thicket of blossoming myrtle,
arbutus, and orange, into the blue of
the Mediterranean. In general, through
France, as the landscape rises the architecture declines. The noblest thing I have
yet seen in the way of Gothic, is seen
rising twelve miles off, over a desolate
and ill-cultivated plain (Chartres Cathedral), while among the noble southern
scenery there is excessively little to
interest in the way of ecclesiastical
architecture, and little appearance of
religion among the people. The ignorance of the lower classes seems about
equal everywhere ; but in the north it is
active, energetic, feeling and enthusiastic,
in the south dull, degraded and slothful.
La Vierge Noire, the presiding Deity

of Chartres Cathedral, is a little black lady about three feet high. The devotion of the whole city to her is quite inexpressible; they are perpetually changing her petticoats, making her presents of pink pincushions, silk reticules, and tallow "dips" by the hundredweight, with occasional silver or plated hearts in cases of especial ingratiation. The group of her worshippers never leaves the cathedral solitary for an instant; she has a priest devoted constantly to her service, who never leaves her altar, and the aisles above her are black with the constant ascent of incense. But in the south they are content with a Mass or two in the course of the day, half said and unheard. The worshippers stagger dreamily into the church, generally lame or weak with some chronic disease, mutter their prayers in the mere fulfilment of peremptory habit, kneel, seemingly without a desire, and rise, seemingly without a hope. At Orleans and Avignon we found small congregations of French Protestants struggling to maintain themselves as congregations against every imaginable disadvantage. If two or three can get together and produce sufficient money to hire a room or build a low chapel, I believe they receive a pittance from the French Government, enough just to maintain a single minister. This poor fellow, who must be both zealous and devoted ever to enter on such a duty, preaches, lectures, prays, and sings, is clerk, reader, and preacher, Sunday after Sunday, to a congregation of perhaps six adults and as many children. A Romanist sometimes saunters in out of curiosity ; he has to do penance for it next time he confesses, and avoids the

door in future, while the Protestant is so
utterly powerless in the way of funds
that he cannot contend with the Romanist
priests with the only argument they are
reluctant to use.   Now and then, nevertheless, he is joined by a stray sheep or
two, and were he well supported, able
to enter into charities of any, even the
slightest extent, or to maintain a tolerably
respectable appearance in the eyes of the
lower classes, he might with real zeal
and good head knowledge, which he
almost always possesses, do much against
the ignorance and laziness of the people
and the priests ;   but with just enough
for himself to pay for a clean shirt and
decent coat on Sundays, and a congregation whose utmost exertion can hardly,
in money matters, whitewash their chapel
and clean its windows, what can he pos-
sibly do against the sweeping invective

and well-supported power of the estab-
lished Church?   It seems to me that we
should be doing far more to advance the
cause of truth, by giving a little support
to these struggling churches, than by
using all our power among howling
savages, and that one of these groups,
crushed and scattered by the Romanist
Church, is more to be lamented than
the continued heathenism of a thousand
Red Indians.   For he who trusts to the
prayers of a black doll for his salvation,
seems to me equally in danger whether it
be called Vushnu or la Vierge; but it is
surely easier to lead the worshipper from
the Mother to the Son, in whom he already
believes, than to raise the conception
of the savage from his rock idol to an
infinite God.

From Nice we went on to Genoa and
Pisa. The coast of the Mediterranean

from Nice to La Spezzia (near which
Shelley was drowned), a run of some
180 miles, is the most glorious combina-
tion of scenery I ever passed through.
Exposed only to the south wind—which
is warm to the hand like the air from a
heated pipe—the palms and aloes wave
over the sea-beach, and rise in blossoming plumes up the promontories of
black marble—crested with white con-
vents and frescoed churches—which the
Maritime Alps fling forward into the
sea ; the valleys are each one grove of
orange, the hill sides shaded with masses
of olive and a wild brushwood of
myrtle and arbutus, and up every chasm
in the hills the eye retires on the inac-
cessible peaks of the higher Alps and
Apennines.   We passed some of this
scenery in a storm of south wind.
Imagine a heavy and wild gale of warm

wind, the sea rising in masses twelve and fifteen feet before they broke, and flinging its foam through the stems of the palm-trees or fifty feet up on the rocks. It tore down three bridges on the road, and some parts of the road itself, and we had great difficulty in getting past. We stayed a fortnight at Florence, which, as a city, disappointed me dreadfully, especially in its churches. Its works of art can disappoint no one, and its population are engaged in active and effective industry, not perhaps in the most profitable industry either to themselves or any one else, being chiefly in cutting precious stones for the Florentine mosaic, about the most costly unison of valuable material with immense human labour that the world produces. We saw a table some three feet across— circular—which had occupied some four

men for six years.   Still it is industry,
and the place looks prosperous, and is
so, I believe, and anything is better
than the *far niente* of Rome.   We
arrived here a month ago, passing, all
the way from Siena, through some of
the ugliest country I ever saw or smelt
in my life, being a compound of volcanic
mud, sulphur, and bilgewater.

St. Peter's I expected to be *disappointed* in.   I was *disgusted.*   The
Italians think Gothic architecture bar-
barous.   I think Greek heathenish.
Greek, by-the bye, it is not, but has
all its weight and clumsiness, without its
dignity or simplicity.   As a whole, St.
Peter's is fit for nothing but a ball-room,
and it is a little too gaudy even for
that, (inside I mean, of course).   But
the overwhelming vastness of every
detail, and the magnificent solidity and

splendour of material are such that, in
walking through it, you think of St.
Paul's as of a pasteboard model—
a child's toy—that the wind may blow
away like a pack of cards and nobody
the wiser. And the exquisite feeling
and glorious art brought out in every
part and *detail* are so impressive that,
were St. Peter's dashed into fifty frag-
ments, I would give our St. Paul's—and
Ludgate Hill into the bargain—for any
one of them. As a whole, I repeat, it is
meagre outside and offensive within. In
the city, if you take a carriage and
drive to express points of lionisation, I
believe that most people of good taste
would expect little and find less. The
Capitol is a melancholy rubbishy square
of average Palladian—modern ; the
Forum, a good group of smashed
columns, just what, if it were got up, as it

very easily might be, at Virginia Water,
we should call a piece of humbug—the
kind of thing that one is sick to death of
in " compositions ; " the Coliseum I have
always considered a public nuisance, like
Jim Crow ; and the rest of the ruins are
mere mountains of shattered, shapeless
brick, covering miles of ground with a
Babylon-like weight of red tiles.   But if,
instead of driving, with excited expecta-
tion, to particular points, you saunter
leisurely up one street and down
another, yielding to every impulse,
peeping into every corner, and keeping
your observation active, the impression
is exceedingly changed.   There is not a
fragment, a stone, or a chimney, ancient
or modern, that is not in itself a study,
not an inch of ground that can be
passed over without its claim of admiration and offer of instruction, and you

return home in hopeless conviction that were you to substitute years for the days of your appointed stay, they would not be enough for the estimation or examination of Rome. Yet the impression of this perpetual beauty is more painful than pleasing, for there is a strange horror lying over the whole city, which I can neither describe nor account for ; it is a shadow of death, possessing and penetrating all things. The sunlight is lurid and ghastly, though so intense that neither the eye nor the body can bear it long ; the shadows are cold and sepulchral ; you feel like an artist in a fever, haunted by every dream of beauty that his imagination ever dwelt upon, but all mixed with the fever fear. I am certain this is not imagination, for I am not given to such nonsense, and, even in illness, never

remember feeling anything approaching
to the horror with which some objects
here can affect me.   It is all like a vast
churchyard, with a diseased and dying
population living in the shade of its
tombstones.   And in fact all the soil
round is black, heavy, and moist ; the
dew lies on it like a sweat.   Wherever
there is a tuft of grass to shade it, if you
take it up in your hand it will not dry,
it seems one mass of accumulated
human corruption.   The population seem
degraded, diseased, unprincipled, and
good-natured in the extreme.   Their
utmost aim is to obtain the capability of
idleness, their highest pleasure to lie
basking in the sun, coiled in their filth,
like lizards.   They will cheat you, lie to
you, rob you, to any extent, without a
thought of its being " incorrect ; " but they
will get wildly fond of you if you treat

them well, and their affection will pre-
vent what their conscience cannot.
Their address is agreeable in the highest
degree, they have all *l'air noble* (unless
broken*   which one-half of
them are) and a perfect specimen of them,
especially if the*   very
magnificent in the way of human nature.
Their intellectual powers are*
highest quality, but *nothing* will induce their exertion. In order, if possible*   my kindly feeling
towards Rome, I took a slight fever a
week ago, some say from sketching in a
damp place, others from a course of
Italian dinners ; but the fever came and
went, and I have been out again and am
all right, only obliged to be excessively
cautious,—in fact I can hardly venture
anywhere, or do anything, though I am

* Space left is where paper was torn under seal.

so used to perpetual checks in all I wish
to do that I feel it less than others
would.   It is not without considerable
bitterness that I can look back on the
three years I spent at the University—
three years of such vigorous life as I
may never know again, sacrificed to a
childish vanity, and not only lost themselves, but breaking down my powers of
enjoyment or exertion, for I know not
how long.   If I ever wished to see the
towers of Oxford again, the wish is
found only in conjunction with another
—Rosalind's—that I had " a thunder-
bolt in mine eye."

Is it not odd that *I*, whose university
life was absurdly, ridiculously exemplary,
and who can safely say that I never,
during those three years, did or said what
I would not have done or said with the
head of my college beside me, should

have this benevolent feeling to my Alma
Mater? Had I devoted a few of the
evening hours which were spent over
Plato to breaking windows in quad or
lamps in the High Street ; had I driven
tandem to Woodstock now and then, instead of attending lecture, and devoted a
little of the money which used to go for
soup tickets and the missionary fund to
paying for the consequent impositions, I
might now have been a respectable B.A.,
with clear eyesight, free chest and
strong limbs, and liberty and power to
go and do where and what I chose.
However, it is perhaps better to lay the
blame on my folly than on my innocence.
I should like, nevertheless, to see the
class system abolished at Oxford. For
those who obtain honours are usually
such as would have been high in scholar-
ship without any such inducement, who

are, in fact, above their trial and take
their position as a matter of course and
a thing of no consequence. To these
the honour is a matter of little
gratification and of less utility. But
the flock of lower standard men of my
stamp, and men below me, who look to
the honour at the end, and strain their
faculties to the utmost to obtain it, not
only have to sustain hours of ponderous
anxiety and burning disappointment,
such as I have seen in some, enough to
eat their life away, but sustain a bodily
and intellectual injury, which nothing
can ever do away with or compensate
for. In this number one may reckon
many of the second class men, who, had
they not been tempted to their own destruction, might have risen afterwards to
a high standard of intellectual power ; but,
just in the hottest moment of boyish

ambition, the University honour is set before them ; and how shall the University
answer for the destruction of intellect,
and even life, consequent on the sudden
struggle ?   I know several advantages of
the class system, but I do not think *one*
which could for a moment be set against
the desolation of a single year.   All this
comes badly from me, because I have been
apparently disappointed in the honours
I am abusing ; but were they all that
I have lost, I believe the utmost chagrin
the loss could cause, would not have
power here to darken the shadow of a
single cypress.

I should have put a date of January 1
in the middle of the last page.   All join
with me in kindest and sincerest wishes
for your health and happiness, and that
of all your family.   I have particularly to
thank you for the loan of the " Pilgrim's

Staff," which we found the most valuable travelling companion of any inmate of the green bag. My mother is especially pleased with it, and it is almost the only book of a devotional character I ever could enjoy. I cannot endure books full of sentences beginning "How" and terminating in a note of admiration.

If you *could* find time to send us a line, informing us of your health and that of Mrs. Dale and your family, you cannot doubt our gratitude. It will be best to send it to Billiter Street, whence it will be forwarded, as I don't know where we are going and not going. I know when I get to Naples I shall have a strong fancy for Athens, but it will be of no use. Best love to Tom and James and Lawford, and all wishes of the season. They make a great fuss about it in St. Peter's—dressing and undressing the Pope all day—and I heard a noble farewell service in one of the parish churches yesterday, and an hour and a half of magnificent organ and chorus —three organs answering each other and the whole congregation joining— as Italians can do always—in perfect melody in parts : the church, a favourable specimen, one blaze of oriental alabaster and gold ; the altar with pillars of lapis lazuli running up fifty feet, more than a foot in diameter, at a guinea an inch in mere material, with groups of white marble flying round and above them, and the roof rising in an apparent infinite height of glorious fresco ; and every possible power of music used to its fullest extent—the best pieces of melody chosen out of standard *operas* and every variety of style, exciting, tender, or sublime—given with ceaseless and overwhelming effect, one solo un-imaginably perfect, by a chosen voice thrilling through darkness. All music *should* be heard in obscurity.

_ I have said nothing of the *art* of Italy, but have bored you quite enough for one while. I will venture to intrude on you again from Naples. — I remain, my dear sir, ever most respectfully yours,

J. RUSKIN.

MY DEAR SIR,

Partly in fear of occupying your time, and partly because there has been little change in my own health, which I could flatter myself would give you any pleasure, I have allowed a long interval to pass since I wrote, during which I have indeed seen much of the external world, but have been altogether prevented by necessary precautions from going into society, or obtaining any knowledge respecting the present state of Italy at all likely to interest you. We spent the early part of the year at Naples, escaping, I hear, a most severe English winter, and coming in for one in Italy which, if less

biting and violent in actual cold, confined us almost altogether to the house
for day after day of crashing rain. The
Neapolitan gutters grew dangerously
ferocious, nearly carrying away their
bridges, and the explosions of steam
from Vesuvius were constant and
glorious. In calm weather the smoke
is amber-coloured, and except at sunrise
or sunset, slightly dull and manufactory-
like, but during rain it is as white as
snow, elastic, voluminous, and dazzling.
We had one or two fine days in the
beginning of March for Pompeii and
Paestum. The first is of course the most
interesting thing in Italy, and particularly pleased me, because I expected
a street and found a city large enough
to lose one's way in. It has been more
knocked about than people are generally
led to suppose : the houses much injured

by earthquake before they were buried, the roofs almost always carried in, and walls shaken and cracked by the weight of the ashes. Modern earthquakes, shiftings of the soil, vineroots from above splitting and displacing the brick-work, and last and worst of all, the care-lessness of the excavators, have reduced the city to a complete ruin; but it is a ruin with all its parts fresh and unde-cayed, and even at the worst, not far differing in aspect from most of the inferior towns of modern Italy, except in the want of their filth and their beggar inhabitants. It is better to talk about Paestum than to see it; a cork model on a good wide mahogany table is about as impressive. I ventured up Vesuvius, for all mountain rides do me good, and found the lava of 1839 still *red* hot to the eye in the daytime, in its hollows,

setting wood on fire, and contributing
greatly to the intellectual enjoyment of
the English by its capabilities in
"roasting of eggs." The crater is at
present a beautifully formed and perfectly
regular funnel, about 300 feet deep, with
a circular hole at the bottom about
twenty or thirty feet over (a rude
guess, for I could not get down to
it), as neatly formed as a well, out of
which the sulphurous smoke springs in
discharges at intervals of about a minute,
with a low murmuring, rising when the
air is still to a height of about 1500 to
2000 feet above the crater in a bright
white column. The whole mass of the
crater, a circle of ashes two miles round,
is warm to the hand, in places painfully
so, and pierced with small holes like
rat-holes, each sending up its small
puffs of smoke. The enormous mass

of sulphurous vapour constantly forced down on Naples has a marked effect on the climate, turning healthy people into hypochondriacs and *vice versâ*. It half killed my father, and did not do me much good, for on the way back to Rome I had the most serious attack of the chest affection I have had at all, blood coming three days running, and once afterwards, and I have been threatened with it at intervals ever since, but still, I think, with some improvement of general health. I was just able to see the Roman festivities, now got up in assistance of the attractions of the rabbit-eating boas in the Surrey zoologicals, and humorously described in the *Times* as occurring on a Festival, of which I fear infallibility itself would confess ignorance, " St. Peter's day at Easter." At Easter they certainly do take place, and on St. Peter's day in June or July, and very pretty things they are in their way. The "Girandole" has got its reputation, and is performing somewhat shabbily under the protection of past years, people still giving it the preference over far finer explosions bestowed constantly on the populace of Paris, but the whole effect of the twenty minutes' burst of changing fire, taking place, as it does, among architectural outlines of the noblest scale and character, and assisted by the roar of the artillery of the fortress, is still unequalled, and I never expect to see any piece of mere spectacle produced by human art fit to be named in the same day with the illumination of St. Peter's.

We left Rome immediately after Easter, and with a little lingering about Venice and Milan to let the snow melt on the Cenis, are now on our road home as fast as I can travel, so that we hope to be in England in about a fortnight.

Since my last attack of blood I have not studied at all. Doctors and my own feelings agree in one point—that hard mental labour of any kind hurts me instantly. I ascribe this to the simple physical fact that during laborious thought the breath is involuntarily held and the chest contracted for minutes together. Whatever causes it, I am obliged, for the present, to give up thought of University or anything else; but I hope when I get home, to be able to get into steady but easy occupation and constant exercise, which may restore my health without entirely wasting the coming years. It is true

that neither air nor exercise have as
yet done much good, but the climate
of Italy never did agree with me,'
and I have been subject to many
causes of slight but constant vexation
from the privations and incapabilities
of ill-health hitherto quite unknown
to me, which have in no small degree
contributed to the increase of their
cause. I have little doubt that perfectly regular habits of life, the direct
contrary of those necessarily induced
by travelling, with fresh air and easy
occupation, will soon restore me. I
have great resources in my drawing—
which, on an easel, requires neither
stooping nor labour of mind—and a
little geology and chemistry may be got
on with without danger, just enough
of Greek to give some steadiness to
the day and keep me ready for taking

my degree when I choose. My sight caused me at first more anxiety than anything else, but as that is not, on the whole, worse, though much tried by glaring sun and a good deal of sketching, I do not trouble myself more about it.

I was very glad to see how instantly Newman submitted to his Bishop in the affair of the Tracts ; however wrong he may be, it is well that he is thus far consistent. I am surprised there has been no more discussion about it, though, by-the-bye, I can hardly judge by the silence of the newspapers, as I hear from Oxford that they are running short of printer's ink, "everybody misunderstanding everybody, and everybody else endeavouring to set them right."

I am sorry they are going so far, for almost every one at Oxford whom I

have had any cause to respect or regard,
has been more or less inclined to favour
their views. Men of high taste and
intellect seem particularly likely to be
led away on their side, while among
their opponents I have found numbers
of the most limited in knowledge and
degraded in feeling, who keep right
only because they do not think enough
to get wrong, and are too conceited
and obstinate to let any one else think
for them. Of course, I am speaking
only of the ordinary disputants of
society, among whom it is somewhat
vexatious to find those who force their
religion down your throat on all
occasions, at all times, with the most
confined views, the most uncharitable
opinions, the worst possible taste, and
the most confirmed, pig-headed self-
conceit, generally in the main right in

what they hold, and the gentle, the spiritual, the high-toned in thought and feeling, unworthy of the surrender of your faith to them for an instant. One may go back, certainly, to the old text, " I have hid these things ; " but it is an unsatisfactory thing for a person beginning a course of divinity to observe that an old woman who can just read has in general more certainty and correctness of faith, and is in far less danger of being led wrong, than the possessor of the most extended know-ledge and cultivated mind, to see that intellect in religion is danger, that knowledge is useless, and an hour of reflection well got over if it has intro-duced no doubt.

By all reports the French Protestant churches are on the increase. At Rome and Naples there are, of course, extensive English congregations during the winter, but quite independent of the inhabitants. They would be the better of a good clergyman in both places. At Naples they sit under one of the coldest dispensers of commonplace moralities that ever was puzzled to get over his half-hour, and at Rome under one of the most intense coxcombs that ever wore dyed whiskers or improved the grammar of the Lord's Prayer. By the-bye, we heard a new reading from the Naples incumbent. : "And lead us! (*not* into temptation)"—a case of comprehensive punctuation worthy of Mattrevis.* Both reverend gentlemen are, I believe, what people call "good creatures," and are certainly quite good enough for their

---

* An allusion to Literature Lectures. See Marlowe's "Edward the Second," act v. scene 5 (Editor's Note).

fashionable congregations, but utterly
incapable of doing any service among
the native population—a population, at
Naples, whose high intellect and kind
disposition are susceptible of almost any
degree of improvement, and are woe-
fully in want of it. At Venice the
British ambassador has service in his
own house, whenever there is a clergyman ready to undertake it, but I believe there is no incumbent; we were
fortunate enough to hear two excellent
flying sermons. There is a French
Protestant service at Turin of the
Vaudois Churches, still, I believe, much
oppressed by the King of Sardinia; they
are compelled not to work on all Romanist
saints' days, can buy no land out of their
own three mountain valleys, and are only
suffered to remain there because under
the protection of England and Prussia.

F

There is still the same striking difference between the Catholic and Romanist cantons of Switzerland, but on the whole, I think, the industry and neatness of the Protestants seem extending beyond their territories. The cleanliness and beauty of Swiss architecture and agriculture is thoroughly exhilarating after the indolence and desolation of Italy. I am sorry to say, however, that neither industry nor Protestantism seem capable of making the Swiss an agreeable people. Knavish in their dealings and brutal in their manners, they often make us regret the loss of the ill-taught but kindly feeling Italian ; and were a stranger to the differences of religion to be introduced successively into one of the churches of Naples and a Protestant Swiss chapel, there can be little doubt which service he would think most acceptable to the Deity — the bowed reverence and brotherly courtesy of the one, or the insolent freedom and animal selfishness of the other. It is but fair to set against this that roads and postmasters seem, beyond all other things and creatures, to be susceptible of the corruptions of Papacy, for the Pope's dominions may be known through all Italy by the roughness of the one and the rascality of the other.

I sincerely hope to find you all in good health when I get to England, when, of course, I shall take the first opportunity of calling, and glad shall I be, after the coldness of foreign services, to find myself again in the pew of St. Bride's, not the same, by-the-bye. I have not been in the church since its reparation. I hope I may not be as much disappointed with it as I was with St. Peter's. It certainly was heavy before, and will be much the better of its lighter colours.

All join in kind regards and best wishes for you and your family. Remember me kindly to Tom and James and Lawford, respectfully to Mrs. Dale. —Ever, my dear sir, most respectfully yours,

J. RUSKIN.

MY DEAR SIR,

I have just received your most kind letter and sit down instantly to reply, with sincere thanks for your permission to write to you at length. Scripture, of course, must be the ultimate appeal, but what I have to say at present is, I think, founded on no solitary passages, but on the broadest and first doctrines of our religion.

I have often wondered, in listening to what are called "practical" discourses from the pulpit, to hear a preacher dividing the duty of *love* into the various minor virtues which affect the present state of men—into gentleness, meekness, sympathy, compassion, almsgiving, and

such like—without ever insisting on the
certain and most important truth, that
as long as we are doubtful of the state
of *one* human soul of those among whom
we dwell, the duty of love claims that
every effort of our existence should be
directed to save that soul, and that in
the present circumstances of humanity,
under which we have every reason for
supposing that the far greater part
of those who die daily in our sight
depart into eternal torment, any direc-
tion of our energies to any one end
or object whatsoever except the saving
of souls, is a merciless and execrable
crime.

Nor can any distinction be made
between laymen and churchmen with
regard to the claims of this duty, but
every one who believes in the name of
Christ is called upon to become a full

and perfect priest. Our daily bread once gained, every faculty of mind and body must be called into full action for this end only, nor can. I think that any one can rightly believe, or be himself in a state of salvation, without holding himself bound, foot, hand, and brain, by this overpowering necessity. Nero's choice of time and opportunity for the pursuit of his musical studies has been much execrated, but is guiltless in comparison to the conduct of the man who occupies himself for a single hour with any earthly pursuit of whatever importance, believing, as he must, if he believe the Bible, that souls which human exertion might save, are meanwhile dropping minute by minute into hell. This being fully granted, the question comes—Are there different means by which such an end can be

attained ? or must we—all who believe—
at once go forth like Paul, tent-making
and preaching for bread and love—I
mean, as far as such sacrifices are consistent with the organisation of society ?
There must be soldiers, merchants,
physicians, members of various necessary
professions, but all these are the representatives in the life of the whole human
species of the hours in the life of an
individual which would be occupied in
obtaining food and raiment. Concerning
these there can be no question. The
doubt is, under what responsibility those
individuals who have leisure lie for its
employment, and how those who have
it in their power to choose their employment are to be regulated in their choice.

They have two questions to ask :
" What means are there by which the
salvation of souls can be attained ? " and

" How are we to choose among them ? "
For instance, does the pursuit of any art
or science, for the mere sake of the
resultant beauty or knowledge, tend to
forward this end ?   That such pursuits
are beneficial and ennobling to our nature
is self-evident, but have we leisure for
them in our perilous circumstances ?   Is it
a time to be spelling of letters, or touching
of strings, counting stars or crystallising
dewdrops, while the earth is failing under
our feet, and our fellows are departing
every instant into eternal pain ?   Or, on
the other hand, is not the character and
kind of intellect which is likely to be
drawn into these occupations, employed
in the fullest measure and to the best
advantage in them ?   Would not great
part of it be useless and inactive
if otherwise directed ?   Do not the
results of its labour remain, exercising

an influence, if not directly spiritual, yet
ennobling and purifying, on all humanity
to all time? Was not the energy of
Galileo, Newton, Davy, Michael Angelo,
Raphael, Handel, employed more effec-
tively to the glory of God in the results
and lessons it has left, than if it had
been occupied all their lifetime in direct
priestly exertion, for which, in all probability, it was less adapted and in which
it would have been comparatively less
effectual?

Yet if the labours of men like these,
who spread the very foundations of
human knowledge to twice their compass,
may be considered as tending to the
great end of salvation, can the same be
said of those who follow their footsteps,
with the average intellect of humanity?
Are not the lives of the greater number
of men employed in the arts and sciences,

as regards their chief duty, wasted? And is it right for any one deliberately to choose such a pursuit as the chief occupation of his life, and abandon the plain duties in which *all* can be of effective service on the very slender chance of becoming a Galileo or a Raphael?

Much more may be said in behalf of general literature, poetry and philosophy, but even here they are only the greatest who can be said to have done any real good, and it may again be doubted how far it is right for any man to devote himself to such pursuits on the chance of becoming a Wordsworth or a Bacon.

Is an individual, then, who has the power of choice, in any degree to yield to his predilections in so important a matter? I myself have little pleasure in the idea of entering the Church, and have been attached to the pursuits of art and science, not by a flying fancy, but as long as I can remember, with settled and steady desire. How far am I justified in following them up? Is it right for any person to enter the Church without any intention of taking active duties upon himself, but that he may be able to preach or minister with authority on any occasion when such ministries may be of immediate and important service?

In all these points I have the more difficulty in coming to a conclusion because I suspect every opinion of being biassed by inclinations. I therefore trouble you, not with a question of mere speculative interest, but with one your answer to which may have much influence in determining my present studies and future course of exertion. I feel, therefore, that under the circumstances, you will think no apology necessary for occupying your time.

I think I am gradually gaining in strength and health. I receive constant testimonies to Jephson's skill and knowledge, and the confidence of the language he holds has at least the good effect of setting my mind at ease. With respectful regards to Mrs. Dale and all your family, believe me ever, my dear sir, most respectfully yours,

J. RUSKIN.

Printed by BALLANTYNE, HANSON & CO.
London & Edinburgh

WORKS BY JOHN RUSKIN.

MODERN PAINTERS. In 5 vols. with all the
Woodcuts, 1 Lithograph, and the 89 Full-Page Steel Engravings. The text is that of the 1873 Edition, with all the
Author's subsequent Notes, and a New Epilogue. Cloth,
6*l*. 6*s*. the 5 vols., imp. 8vo.

ON THE OLD ROAD: a Collection of Miscellaneous
Pamphlets, Articles, and Essays (1834–84). In 3 vols.,
including—My First Editor, Lord Lindsay's Christian Art,
Eastlake's History of Oil Painting, Samuel Prout, Sir Joshua
and Holbein, Pre-Raphaelitism, Opening of the Crystal Palace,
Study of Architecture, The Cestus of Aglaia, Minor Writings
upon Art, Notes on Science, Fiction, Fair and Foul, Fairy
Stories, Usury, Home and its Economies, The Lord's Prayer,
An Oxford Lecture, &c. 8vo, cloth, 30*s*. the 3 vols. (Not sold
separately.)

ARROWS OF THE CHACE: being a collection of
the Scattered Letters of John Ruskin. With added Preface by
the Author. Published chiefly in the Daily Newspapers during
the Years 1840–80. In 2 vols. cloth, 8vo, 20*s*. the 2 vols. (Not
sold separately.)

PROSERPINA: Studies in Wayside Flowers. Vol. I.,
containing 13 Full-Page Illustrations from Wood and Steel.
Cloth, 10*s*. The first Four Parts of Vol. II. are also to be had,
each 1*s*. 8*d*., 8vo.

THE LAWS OF FESOLE: a Familiar Treatise on
the Elementary Principles and Practice of Drawing and
Painting. As determined by the Tuscan Masters. Vol. I.,
containing 12 Full-Page Steel Engravings, cloth, 8*s*., 8vo.

PRÆTERITA. Outlines of Scenes and Thoughts perhaps Worthy of Memory in my Past Life. Vols. I. and II. of this autobiography now ready, in cloth, 13*s*. 8vo.

FORS CLAVIGERA: Letters to the Labourers and Workmen of Great Britain, in 8 vols. and Index vol. 7*s*. each, 8vo.

"OUR FATHERS HAVE TOLD US": Sketches of the History of Christendom. Part I. The BIBLE of AMIENS. With 4 Steel Engravings and Plan of the Western Porches of Amiens Cathedral. Cloth, 6*s*., 8vo.

THE ART OF ENGLAND. Lectures delivered at Oxford in 1883. I. Rossetti and Holman Hunt—II. E. Burne-Jones and G. F. Watts—III. Sir F. Leighton and Alma Tadema—IV. Mrs. Allingham and Miss Kate Greenaway—V. John Leech and J. Tenniel—VI. George Robson and Copley Fielding—VII. Appendix and Index. Cloth, 6*s*., 4to.

UNTO THIS LAST. Four Essays on the First Principles of Political Economy. Eighth Edition. Cloth, 3*s*.; roan, gilt edges, 12mo. 4*s*.

SELECTIONS FROM RUSKIN. Vol. I. with Engraved Portrait after George Richmond's picture, 540 pages. 6*s*. Crown 8vo.

Scenes of Travel, Characteristics of Nature, Painting and Poetry, Painters and Pictures, Architecture and Sculpture, Ethical and Didactic Subjects.

Vol. II. with Photogravure Portrait from a recent photograph, 500 pages, 6*s*. Crown 8vo.

Art, Education, Ethics, Economy, Religion.

SESAME and LILIES. A Small Edition, containing only the Two Lectures, "King's Treasures," and "Queen's Gardens," and a New Preface. Thirteenth Edition. Crown 8vo, cloth, 5*s*.; roan, gilt edges, 7*s*. 6*d*.—The larger complete edition, cloth, 9*s*. 6*d*.

Crown 8vo, cloth, each 5s.; roan, gilt edges, each 7s. 6d.

MUNERA PULVERIS. Six Essays on the Elements of Political Economy.

TIME and TIDE, by WEARE and TYNE. Twenty-five Letters to a Working Man of Sunderland on Laws of Work.

The CROWN of WILD OLIVES. Four Essays on Work, Traffic, War, and the Future of England. With Articles on the Economy of the Kings of Prussia. Fifth Edition.

QUEEN of the AIR: a Study of the Greek Myths of Cloud and Storm.

The TWO PATHS. Lectures on Art and its Application to Decoration and Manufacture. Delivered in 1858–59. With New Preface and Added Notes.

"A JOY FOR EVER" (and its Price in the Market). The Substance of Two Lectures on the Political Economy of Art. With New Preface and Added Articles.

The EAGLE'S NEST. Ten Lectures on the Relation of Natural Science to Art.

LECTURES on ART, delivered at Oxford in 1870. Revised by the Author, with New Preface. Fifth Edition.

The ETHICS of the DUST. Ten Lectures to Little Housewives on the Elements of Crystallisation. Sixth Edition.

The ELEMENTS of DRAWING. In Three Letters to Beginners. Illustrated.

www.ingramcontent.com/pod-product-compliance
Lightning Source LLC
Chambersburg PA
CBHW030631270326
41927CB00007B/1392